D1644118

Always
Plenty

Always Plenty

Caroline Rose Kraft

Based on the true story, with permissions from Eddie Smith Ogan. Original story by Eddie Smith Ogan, published at mikeysfunnies.com.

ALWAYS PLENTY

ISBN 0-692-66332-0

For Daddy and Mommy,
who raised me rich in love.
And for Eddie.

Chapter One

"Are they frozen, Eddie?" Ocy asked.

Eddie gingerly touched the sleeve of one of Mom's aprons, hanging stiff and crisp as bark on a birch tree. It was early spring in North-Eastern Washington State. The two girls were behind their small home, examining a rickety clothesline.

"Yeah, they're still frosty," she replied without looking at her sister. "And they will stay frosty all day by the looks of things."

The two girls, tall and slender for their ages, strained their necks skyward. The March sun was more of a smudge than a blaze, and the clouds looked murky and thick.

"Let's bring them in then," Ocy suggested after a moment. "We have to wear those stockings tomorrow, and stockings are supposed to keep you warm."

Eddie's hazel eyes twinkled.

"I know what we should do!" She yanked the apron off the line with a bounce. "Here! Help me get everything down, fast as you can, and follow me!"

Ocy, whose name was said like "Oh see," was used to following her sister, Eddie. Eddie was two years older and seemed almost grown up. The two girls gathered the laundry off the line in a big, frigid bundle and rushed up the stoop and into the house. Mom and

Darlene had gone to visit Mrs. Estes from church. Mrs. Estes was a widow who used to ride the rails with her two sons during the depression. She would go from town to town, they say, looking for work or a hot plate of food. Eventually, she had to let her cousin adopt her children, and she got a job working on a hay farm as a cook. Now Mrs. Estes was penniless and all alone in the world, for even her sons had been lost in the war. Darlene would darn her clothes and wash her dishes while Mom helped her wash her long, white hair. Mrs. Estes couldn't pay for their work, and wasn't enough in her right mind to know to do so, but Mom always said, "Who needs money when you have friends?" Mrs. Estes lived to be ninety-seven that way.

The two sat on the rag-rug inside the front door and took their boots off. Eddie's boots flung across the room, as they were a friend's old pair and still much too big. Ocy's boots stubbornly slid off after a fight. They had been too small for some time now. They rushed through the small family room, past the radio, the medicine cabinet and the round portrait of their beloved father who had passed away five years earlier. Mom had her own small bedroom where the girls also kept their school things, and Darlene, Eddie and Ocy shared the other room. The window was decorated with frost crystals like pine needles and stars, and the floor creaked.

Ocy followed Eddie's lead as they hoisted the bare, blue-and-white striped mattress off the rickety frame.

"Put the stockings under here!" she ordered with a grin.

Ocy did so, along with Darlene's icy slip.

They replaced the mattress and threw the pillows back on the way they had been. There were two pillows and Ocy always slept in the crack.

Ocy smiled, wide-eyed as she surveyed their work, then they both went about putting the other things away and soaking the beans as Mom had asked them to.

"Can you believe it's only a month until Easter?" Eddie was sitting at the kitchen table, studying for her geometry exam while Ocy stirred the beans.

"Oh my Sainted Aunt!" Ocy whipped around, spoon in hand. "Is it really? I can't wait for the parade!"

"Yes!" Eddie slammed her pencil inside her book. "And flowers in all the shop windows on Main Street and..." She was going to say "chocolate," but she remembered that last year they hadn't been able to afford any. "And going to church and singing 'Blest Be the Tie' while Mr. Eager plays his harp," she quickly added.

Ocy gave a big, Ocy smile and turned thoughtfully back to her bean pot.

Just then, Mom and Darlene burst in, scarves flying.

"Brrr!" Mom whinnied. "And they call this 'Spring'!"

"How was Mrs. Estes?" Eddie ran to help her mother out of her long, woolen coat.

"She is quite well," the shivering woman answered. "We got her fire going before we left and fed her chickens. Don't let me forget to check on her again in the next few days. The weather is bitter."

Darlene unwrapped the scarf she'd worn around her stylish hair and immediately put on her own apron. Their two older sisters and both brothers had already gotten married, moved out, and started their families. It was up to Darlene now to keep Mom and "the little girls," as she called them, cared for.

"You'd better finish studying," she warned Eddie, eyebrows raised. "Tomorrow's Sunday."

Darlene opened the pot and took a whiff of the beans, now boiling.

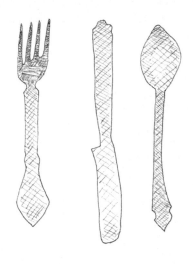

Chapter Two

"Where in this earth are my stockings?" Darlene was whirling around the little house like a tornado.

Ocy gasped and caught Eddie's eye. Eddie ran into their bedroom and lifted up a corner of the mattress and pulled the stockings out as fast as if she were retrieving them from the jaws of a wild dog. Just as she had hoped, their sleeping bodies had kept them warm under there all night. There was a bit of a puddle under the bed where a particularly icy sock had thawed, and they were wrinkled as your grandma's grandma, but they weren't frozen anymore! The girls laughed and laughed as they put them on and marveled at their "invention." Dad used to say, "necessity is the mother of invention," and Eddie wondered what he had meant. The necessity of what?

Eddie and her sisters hurriedly dressed for church and left with no breakfast, partially because they didn't want to be late and partially because, though the girls paid no mind, there was nothing in the house to eat but the beans they were going to warm for lunch. When they got to church, Brother Zeb greeted them at the big, white doorway with a kindly smile. There was a large, yellow ribbon on the front door of the church to honor Brother Zeb's nephew Henry who was still missing. It was March 24, 1946 and the state of Washington was still feeling softhearted toward those who had been touched by the recent World War.

The family of four took their seats and opened their hymnals. Out of the corner of her eye, Eddie could see some girls from her class at school watching them. One of them whispered something about "Eddie" being a boy's name. Eddie focused her eyes on the hymnal, though she knew the words by heart. Her father had chosen her name, convinced she was going to be another boy, and she wouldn't change it for the world! Sure, her real name was Edna, but to her family she had always been and would always be just "Eddie." Some of those girls passed their dresses to Ocy, and she was happy to wear them. Sometimes Eddie and Ocy marveled that they would part with such pretty things, simply because they needed a little patch or a couple new buttons.

None of the girls from Eddie's class could pass dresses to her now. She was already taller than Mom and well on her way to being as tall as her teacher, Mr. Grant.

Brother Zeb delivered a fine sermon, and afterward, he made an important announcement. He asked the church to collect a special Easter offering for a particularly poor family in their congregation. Eddie listened intently as he asked everyone to "give sacrificially" in order that the family might be blessed by their generosity. Ocy and Eddie smiled at each other. It sounded like a challenge. Almost like a secret mission! Immediately Eddie's mind began running a hundred miles an hour.

Eddie walked backward, facing her family,

almost all the way home.

"What do you think?" she asked Mom. "Could we put a little money aside for the poor family?"

Mom's eyes lit up under her gray hat.

"Anything is possible!" was her bright reply. "I think we should go to the market tomorrow and buy potatoes...lots of potatoes."

The girls all exchanged excited looks. Mom was hatching a plan.

"We could live on potatoes for the next month and save maybe...twenty dollars on our grocery bill!"

Ocy's mouth fell open at the idea of having twenty whole dollars at once.

"Wonderful!" Eddie nearly tripped over an old bottle. "That's a lot!"

Darlene pulled her scarf away from her shivering mouth.

"I can babysit and take as many cleaning jobs as I can find." She spoke as more ideas came into her mind. "And...for twenty cents, you can buy enough cotton loops to make three potholders. I'll bet we could sell those three-for-a-dollar!"

The family bustled to the side of the road while a shiny, blue Ford sped past.

"I know!" Ocy burst out, her two braids bobbing. "We can keep the lights off as much as possible and not use the radio...at all! How much would that save on our electric bill, Mom?"

"Good thinking!" Mom cheered. "That could save us a pretty penny, Ocy!"

Everyone was beaming by the time they got home, so much so that they scarcely noticed the dropping temperatures. As soon as they got inside, Darlene climbed up on a rickety chair and pulled a big pickle jar off the shelf.

"We'll collect the money in this," she announced, placing it in the center of the table.

"If it will all fit!" Ocy interrupted.

Everyone laughed and folded their arms and gazed at the empty jar.

"Who knows how much we can collect in a whole month!" Mom said.

Darlene put the beans on the stove and Eddie set the table. Two soup bowls, a little mixing bowl, and a big coffee cup that had been Dad's would do for today's meal. Ocy held out a handful of silverware and everyone selected their utensil with their other hand over their eyes.

"Fork!" Mom stated proudly as she made her blind selection.

"Spoon!" Darlene announced.

"Spoon again!" Eddie decreed.

"Butter knife!" Ocy declared, as she opened her hand to all that was left. "Just as I suspected!"

Everyone giggled all through lunch.

Chapter Three

Eddie and Darlene walked down the dirt road toward their house. Darlene pulled the red bandana off her head and wiped her face. Her curls sprung around her face. It had been a hard day's work at Mrs. MacLachlan, cleaning and digging roots out of the flowerbeds. Eddie carried her muddy apron in a wad.

"Well," Eddie said after a long, tired pause. "That's five more dollars for the jar."

She felt more excited than she sounded,

but it took all her breath just to keep walking.

"Yup!" Her older sister raised an eyebrow. "Which makes sixteen dollars and seventy-five cents."

"And..." Eddie bent and scratched an itch through her stocking. "We're not done yet!"

By now they were approaching the whitewashed front porch of their home. The two tired girls slowly scaled the steps, pressing down on their knees. Ocy was waiting for them at the screen door, her hair tied in pincurls.

"Seven!" she announced proudly.

"Seven what?" Darlene asked, hanging her handbag on the hook.

"Potholders!" She motioned toward a tidy little pile on the coffee table. The cotton loops they had purchased yesterday had magically turned into seven neat little potholders, ready for the market.

"Oh, great!" The two eldest girls forgot how tired they were. "They look dandy, Ocy!"

All week they had rushed home from school and put their books away, quick as brown foxes, before rushing back into town. They had knocked on doors, offered to clean and work in the yard and babysit. On Wednesday, Ocy had cleaned all afternoon for old Mr. Eager from church, and on Thursday night, Darlene had babysat the six Montgomery children. On Friday, they went and bought the cotton loops for the potholders.

Immediately, Darlene and Eddie sat down on the old sofa and started making potholders, their fingers moving like spiders spinning webs. They estimated they had enough loops for twenty potholders, and with seven already completed, there were only thirteen to go. Every three potholders represented a whole dollar if they could sell them, and they were certain they could!

Oftentimes, they used to listen to the radio while they worked, but since they weren't using the radio all month to save on the electric bill, Eddie started them singing. Ocy and Darlene chimed in with their best impersonations of the Andrews Sisters. Mostly they just laughed, which was it's own kind of music.

The next week whizzed by. The three girls and their mother couldn't remember ever laughing so much, working so much, or being so excited about anything. Every night, before they turned off the lamp, they gathered around the kitchen table and counted all the money in the pickle jar, even if they hadn't made any more that day. They looked at the pickle jar as if it were a magic genie's lamp and dreamt aloud about what the poor family might use the money for. Even Mom would clasp her hands together and sigh.

"Maybe they need food for the baby," Darlene suggested.

"Or some seeds for their spring garden!" Eddie added.

"Maybe they don't have enough money to write to their family," Mom wondered, almost to herself.

"I hope the jar is enough for whatever it is they need," Ocy sighed.

"I'm sure it will be!" Mom gave her a squeeze around the shoulders and turned the lamp out with a little turn of the knob.

Darlene and Ocy went to bed first. Eddie stayed up looking out the window at the moon. It was a cloudy night, and it looked to her as if the Man in the Moon was peeking at her from around a wispy, lace curtain. She stared at the moon for what seemed like a long time, praying in her heart for the poor family. Soon she got too cold, so she jumped into bed with her sisters. The small, blue and white striped mattress never seemed warm enough until they were all under the quilt together.

Chapter Four

It was only a week until Easter now, and the three girls were gathering their things for church. The family Bible, the gray scarf that used to be Dad's that Mom always wore on particularly cold days, Eddie's other boot. They were about to run out the door when Ocy turned back.

"Wait, wait!" She hollered, stampeding into the kitchen.

She took hold of the pickle jar, sitting on

the table and gave it a loud kiss, before hiding it safely in the coffee cabinet.

"Oh, Ocy!" Darlene and Eddie said in unison. "Let's go, let's go!"

They hustled down the stoop and down the road. Brother Zeb was still greeting the congregation at the front door.

"Good morning, ladies!" Brother Zeb said warmly, his rosy cheeks glowing against the wind.

"Good morning!" Mom said with a nod.

"Good morning!"

"Good morning!" Darlene and Eddie echoed.

"Would you like to buy a potholder?" Ocy asked, pulling a nice red one out of her coat pocket.

"Ocy! Shush!" Mom tugged at her youngest daughter's coat, and they hurried to find their seats.

Brother Zeb just let out a bellowing laugh.

During church, all Eddie could think about was who the family might be and how much money the rest of the church had gathered by then. Brother Zeb had asked for everyone to give "sacrificially." She looked around casually counting heads. There were about eighty other people in the church, including children. She estimated that whatever they were able to raise, the rest of the church would be able to collect at least twenty times as much! This gave her goose bumps. She spun around grinning to face Brother Zeb again, but she caught the eye of those same girls from her class. They were whispering and passing around a catalog. She knew they were showing each other which dresses and bonnets they had ordered for Easter. It seemed to be all those silly girls thought about this time of year! In the summer, it would be nothing but where they were going to vacation and which swimsuits were fashionable. Eddie blinked hard as if to clear her mind and turned the pages of the Bible to keep up with the sermon.

On Monday morning, the sun came out and melted the icicles, which was good because the girls had work to do. Darlene and Mom had to go to Widow Estes' first thing that morning to help her wash her hair and do her laundry. After that, they were going to answer an ad in the paper for someone who needed a fence painted. They were probably competing with men for the job, but Darlene and Mom were tall and strong and knew they could do the work if given the chance.

"Eddie?" Ocy was stuffing nice, new potholders into a brown grocery bag. "What if no one wants to buy the potholders? I mean, we've already made 'em and we can't give the yarn back to the store now."

"O ye of little faith!" Eddie's eyes were wide. "I'm sure everyone will want one! They are so beautifully done, especially those that Mom made. And everyone uses pots and needs potholders. Besides, God wouldn't want us to waste our money and not have those dollars to put in the jar, would He?"

"No," Ocy spoke slowly, still looking at the grocery bag. "I don't suppose so. The family really needs the money, and God knows that."

"Right!" Eddie offered her a hand up. "So all we have to do is show people how they can help! If we want to sell all the rest today, we'd better get going."

The two girls left the house with springs in

their steps. Well, Eddie would've had a spring in her step if her shoes weren't a couple sizes too big. Eddie shuffled with the bag of potholders, and Ocy skipped ahead, her braided pigtails shining in the morning light.

Somehow, it didn't seem right to start at the nearest house. The girls decided to head into the center of town and work their way out. They would start at Mr. Eager's house. They thought he was the nicest old man in town and might give them a boost. Mr. Eager was a widower, and had been for many years. He was perfectly happy to cook his own meals, so they heard, and could be in need of a potholder! Mr. Eager not only cooked, but he also played the harp beautifully. He was a sailor in the navy and had a schnauzer named Shrimp.

Mr. Eager's house set back from Main

Street just a bit behind an empty lot where the old post office had burned down. It was visible from the church across the street. The girls ambled up his driveway with butterflies in their stomach. If Mr. Eager bought one, or dare they hope two potholders, they'd already feel like millionaires. That would mean sixty-six more cents for the pickle jar and only eighteen potholders left to sell.

Eddie handed Ocy the bag and knocked on the door. Shrimp howled like a lonely coyote inside. Soon Mr. Eager opened the door, already smiling.

"Why hello, ladies!" He exclaimed, merrily. "How can I help you?"

Suddenly Eddie got the feeling she was taking advantage of Mr. Eager. They had specifically chosen his house first because he was so kind. Maybe that wasn't fair.

"Hi, Mr. Eager!" she managed to say. "We were just...we didn't want to bother you, but..."

Shrimp started to lick her leg, and she looked down as her voice trailed off. Just then, Ocy spoke up:

"We are selling genuine, handmade potholders to raise money for the sacrificial offering at church! Would you like to buy one... or two?" She reached into the sack and pulled out a thick, blue potholder.

It was one of the potholders Mom had made, and it was very nice. Eddie began to regain her pride in their product. She thought about the proverb from the Bible which Mom had read aloud just that morning, "She perceiveth that her merchandise is good."

"My, my!" Mr. Eager took hold of the pretty potholder with two, bony fingers. "These look like fine quality!"

Eddie and Ocy exchanged quick, satisfied grins.

"My sisters and mother and I spent a long time making them," Eddie put in. "And we're selling them three-for-a-dollar...to put toward the offering for the poor family."

"Three-for-a-dollar, you said?" Mr. Eager used another, shaky finger to pull the bag open and peer inside. "In that case...I'll take three!"

The girls left Mr. Eager's house with a whole dollar and a lot more confidence in their business! They patted Shrimp on the head and gave Mr. Eager a curtsy and put the money in a little green purse Eddie was wearing inside her coat.

When they returned home that evening, Mom and Darlene were already cooking the potatoes for dinner. The orange sun was sliding down behind the rooftops and Eddie's big shoes had rubbed blisters through her stockings. Ocy was still holding the brown grocery sack, but now it was folded up and stuck under one arm. Her braids were fuzzy, and Eddie's curls had all but given up on being curly.

Mom opened the door and stood with one foot inside the house and one foot on the porch.

"So?" she asked. "Did you have any luck?"

Ocy began to smile and turned to Eddie.

"I guess you could say that," Eddie grinned. "We were having to turn down customers on our way home!"

Chapter Five

It was Easter-Eve, as Ocy called it, and she and Eddie were on a thrilling errand. Saturday morning had dawned, cold and crisp. The sun was doing its best job at shining, but it was still nippy as the sisters stepped briskly down the street. Eddie was hugging a pickle jar as if it were her own dear baby, and Ocy was following close behind as if she was worried it might wake up and wonder where she was. They didn't run, but they did hurry and soon they were at JACK'S GROCERS AND MEAT MART. Eddie tried to act calm. She was too old to be giddy in public, she felt. This idea never crossed Ocy's mind; and, as soon as she held the door open for Eddie and leapt inside, she clasped her hands together and gave a little shriek of delight. Eddie paid no heed and walked directly to the service counter.

"Good morning, Mr. Jack." Her head was tilted downward under her little brown cap, and her olive eyes looked big and serious.

"Good morning, Edna!" He pressed his palms on the counter and surveyed his two newest customers. "I haven't seen you ladies in a while!"

"We've been living on potatoes!" Ocy offered.

"Mighty smart," Mr. Jack had to admit.

"How can I help you today?"

"We need to exchange...this." Eddie hoisted the pickle jar onto the counter. "For bills."

Mr. Jack spun the jar around and examined it carefully.

"I see!" he said. "Are you planning on taking a trip? Buying a new car, perhaps?"

The girls giggled, and Ocy assured him that was not the case.

"We saved all this up," Eddie said in a low voice, for propriety's sake. "For the poor family from church. Brother Zeb is having the whole congregation save up for a special Easter offering for a poor family."

She felt a little silly explaining this to a grown man, but she knew Mr. Jack didn't go to church. Somehow, she always managed to pretend that she didn't know that, but when you go to the same church your whole life, it's almost impossible to not notice who is or isn't there every Sunday.

"Ah, I see!" he said again. "That's mighty charitable of you all."

He spun around and began to count the money on the back counter. Eddie and Ocy forgot all about being grown up when they were on their way home. The faster one ran, the faster the other found her own feet flying. In no time, they were inside their house and at the kitchen table. They hadn't even thought to take the pickle jar home, they were too eager to show the cash to Mom and Darlene.

"Just look!" Eddie exclaimed. "Have you ever seen so much money?" She gingerly laid the bills on the table.

"Not for a long, long time," Mom said, gazing dreamily at the crisp paper.

"Three twenties..." Darlene watched the

money coming out of the purse. "And a ten! All look mint-new!"

"I can't wait to put it in the offering plate tomorrow." Eddie breathed.

"Mom told me I could do it!" Ocy said, not meaning to be rude, but just as eager as Eddie.

"We'll all do it!" Mom said, with a laugh. "There's plenty to go around!"

"There sure is!" Darlene put her hands on her face and shook her head.

That night, Mom turned on the radio, and everyone danced. They kept the lamps on and talked about the poor family and what a happy Easter they were going to have. They coiled the money in Mom's change purse and prepared everything for the next morning. Finally, they went to bed, but no one slept much at all. They had no new Easter dresses or Easter bonnets, but they didn't mind. They had had so much fun saving and raising the money and now it was almost time for the grand finale. That was better than any old bonnet.

The moon was gleaming through the tattered lace in the window of the girls' bedroom. The radio seemed happy to be singing again, even though it was turned off again now, along with the lights. Even still, music and light seemed to linger in the air. The money was safe in Mom's purse, and the last few potatoes sat in the kitchen cabinet. Somewhere, a poor family was preparing for Easter, and they were in for a big surprise. Eddie rolled over again and pulled the old quilt over her shoulder. It sounded like Darlene and Ocy were finally asleep. She said one more prayer for the poor family and drifted off.

Chapter Six

The sun rose on Easter Sunday, but it was impossible to see it. Clouds had swept in overnight and brought heavy rain. By the time the family was ready to step out, puddles had crept up around the stoop and the sky was the color of charcoal. The three girls and their mother scarcely seemed to notice this change in the weather. They were too excited about the special offering and the contents of the little coin purse. They didn't own an umbrella, and the walk to church was over a mile, but they cheerfully marched on.

Darlene had to stop a couple of times to read-just her shoes. They had cardboard in them to patch the holes, but the cardboard had come apart and rainwater flooded in. When she looked down, water poured out of her hat, and before they stepped inside the church, Ocy had to wring her mittens out in the flow-erbed!

Smiling as they went, the dripping family took their seats near the front of the church. Had it really been a month since the day Broth-er Zeb announced the Easter offering? Most of the other families had come in cars, or at least with umbrellas, and were not nearly so wet. Eddie twisted around and saw several girls from school. They each wore a different pastel shade, reminding her of candy. Their dresses were new and ruffled and matched their fashionable hats. They even had new gloves and small, matching purses.

Eddie turned back around and tried to hide a smile. If only they knew what was in her mom's coin purse that morning! She felt as rich as a duchess. Brother Zeb gave a wonderful sermon on the resurrection of Christ, Mr. Eager's skillful fingers strummed the harp; before long, it was time for the offering plate to be passed around. The girls' mother opened her little purse and passed the bills down. When the plate came by, their mom put a ten-dollar bill in and let the three girls each add a twenty. Eddie closed her eyes and imagined the plate traveling from pew to pew behind her, collecting more and more money. She wondered if the poor family was at church that morning, and she wondered how much money would be collected.

On the way home from church, the sunshine peeked through the dripping tree branches. They sang all the way home, laughing and skipping and feeling as light as dandelion seeds. When they got home, Mom had a surprise for them. She had bought a dozen eggs and they had boiled Easter eggs, along with the last of the potatoes, for lunch!

"This really must be the best Easter we've had in five years," Darlene said late that afternoon.

She was gazing at a picture of their dad, hanging above the radio. Just then, headlights flashed across their front windows. It was Brother Zeb's car, and it was parked in front of their gate. The girls exchanged confused glances. It wasn't like Brother Zeb to pop in on them, and they imagined he was celebrating Easter with his family.

Mom went to the door and she and Brother Zeb had a short, quiet exchange. Before long at all, the girls heard them say their goodbyes, and Brother Zeb walked down the steps and drove away. Mom shut the door and walked silently to the kitchen table where her three daughters sat with a game of Checkers on hold. She was holding an envelope.

"What's that?" Eddie asked. The look on Mom's face made her uneasy.

Mom said nothing. She just opened the envelope and spilled its contents on the table. Out fell three crisp twenty-dollar bills, a ten-dollar bill and seventeen one-dollar bills. Ocy separated them with her fingers, her mouth wide open. Eddie stared at the money as if she were blind. Darlene stared at Mom's face, but Mom's face said nothing. After a moment,

Mom put all the money back in the envelope. Darlene, Eddie and Ocy looked at the floor. No one said a word. The girls had gone from feeling like millionaires on top of the world to feeling like poor nobodies. Eddie thought about what a happy life she had had. It had been a terrible time when Dad died, but they had found much to be thankful for even since then. She had always felt sorry for kids who didn't have her wonderful mom and dad, her own brothers and sisters and a home where friends were always welcome.

She thought for a long time, staring at her too-big shoes under the kitchen table. The checked floor was scuffed and faded, but it was clean. The checkers lay forgotten on the old tablecloth. She suddenly felt so strange. So different. For the first time in her life, she felt truly poor. Sure, she had always known they didn't have everything everyone else had, but she had never felt sorry for herself, or for her sisters or Mom. She had never thought it was that bad, just the way things were. She thought about her striped mattress with no sheets, about Dad's tattered, gray scarf that Mom wore. The other mothers were wearing the latest styles. Some of them had a scarf to match every dress. Eddie's head began to spin. She didn't want to think about it...any of it, anymore.

What's the point? She thought as she silently scooped the checkers back into their box. She felt stupid. Everyone at school knew they were poor. Everyone at church had probably known they were poor all along. Brother Zeb just said so. Eddie walked into her bedroom to put the game away and caught a glimpse of herself in the old mirror which hung next to the window. The mirror was small, but she could see enough. She could see her hair, which had been drenched by rain that morning and dried again. It hadn't been protected by a nice hat or an umbrella or the roof of a car. She could see the color of her dress, probably eight years old now. It had belonged to someone before Darlene had worn it, and Darlene wore it for several seasons. She could see her eyes, and when she saw them, she could only see them for a moment, for tears sprung into them and all was a blur.

Eddie sat on the edge of the little bed with the blue striped mattress and willed herself not to cry. There was no sound from the other room where her family sat silently. Tomorrow was another day, another week. She immediately knew she didn't want to go to school. At school, everyone already knew...had known all along. She felt suddenly ashamed of her clothes, her family, herself. She was in the ninth grade. Legally, you only had to go through the eighth grade, so Eddie decided right then she would drop out. No need to face that school again.

Eddie didn't want to think about it anymore, but that's all she did until finally the light faded from her room and the sun fell from her window. She took her dress off and crawled into bed, not even bothering to say goodnight to anyone. Soon her sisters joined her. A few minutes later, she heard her mother retreat to her bedroom. No words were spoken.

Chapter Seven

The next morning, the mood had not changed. Eddie, usually one to bounce out of bed and eagerly start her day, watched from beneath the quilt as Darlene and Ocy prepared for school. She decided if they were going, she might as well go too. They might need her. Besides, Mom would want her to go. With this thought, she hoisted herself up and got dressed.

Mom served fried potatoes for breakfast

and told them to have a good day, but there was no chatting or laughing like most mornings. They walked glumly to school and back that day, and every day that week. They did their work, but they hardly spoke a word to anyone. Eddie kept her shoes close to her desk so no one would look at them and see how large and old they were. Darlene didn't stop and talk to the other girls walking home as she used to do. Even Ocy, usually such a chatterbox, pulled her coat up around her neck and hurried home every day. Her teacher asked if she would like to stay after class and help clean out her desk for a nickel. Ocy declined politely and pertly. What use had she for a nickel?

Finally, after a miserably long week, Saturday came. Eddie didn't want to think about last Saturday when the sun shone and Mr.

Jack exchanged their pickle jar of money. She didn't want to think about anything, so she just stuck her nose in her geometry book and tried not to think at all.

"Well," Mom said from the kitchen table. Her voice sounded so loud compared to the silence they had become used to. "What in this world are we going to do?"

Darlene was staring wistfully out the window, as if the clothesline were something interesting to look at.

"About what?" she asked.

"About the money, of course." Mama pulled the envelope out of her apron pocket.

Ocy looked at Eddie. Eddie shrugged.

"I...I don't know." Eddie said feebly. "What do poor people do with money?"

Mama pursed her lips together and put the envelope back in her apron. Nothing more was said about it. The next morning before Eddie got out of bed, she heard Darlene and Mom talking in the kitchen.

"We're going to church," Mom was saying. "And that's final."

Darlene rushed into the room and began dressing as if Eddie and Ocy weren't there. No one said "good morning," and it would've felt rude, only no one felt like replying anyway. They all felt the same. They didn't want to go church today. They never wanted to go to church again. They were the poor family at church, and they didn't want to face it.

It was a sunny morning, so unlike Easter morning, but the girls didn't speak at all. They walked in a straight line. Mom started to sing a line from a song they all liked, but no one joined in. Soon, her voice faded away.

When the family settled back into their

second-row seats, no one looked around to see what anyone else was wearing. They looked up to see Brother Zeb, but instead they saw a man they had never seen before. He greeted the church and began to tell them about his life as a missionary to an African tribe. Eddie's eyes felt glued to him. Being a missionary sounded exciting. Her heart began to beat faster.

He told them of how the African people built their churches out of sun-dried bricks. Finally, he said, "For one hundred dollars, we can buy a roof for this newest church, where our brothers and sisters in Africa can safely worship! Can't we all sacrifice to help these poor people?"

Suddenly, Eddie felt as if she had been awakened from a trance. She looked at Mom, and Mom was already smiling. Ocy and Darlene smiled too. It was the first any of them had smiled since Brother Zeb had stopped by a week ago. Mom reached into her purse and pulled out the envelope. She passed it to Darlene. Darlene gave it to Eddie, and Eddie handed it to Ocy. Ocy laid the whole envelope in the offering plate when it came by.

When the offering was counted, Brother Zeb happily announced that it was a little over a hundred dollars. The missionary was thrilled! He hadn't expected such a large offering from the small church. He said, "You must have some rich people in this church!"

Suddenly, it struck Eddie! She had given eighty-seven of that "little over one hundred dollars"! She and Mom and Darlene and Ocy had given that money! They were the rich family in the church this time! After church, they walked home in pure bliss, singing all the way. They didn't notice the other girls walking home in their pretty dresses and new hats. They were too busy feeling like millionaires again!

"You know," Eddie said as they approached their small house. "Money doesn't make you rich. Riches are your Mom and Dad, your brothers and sisters, friends and good times."

"And Jesus!" Ocy added.

"And so many other things." Mama said, hanging the old gray scarf on the hook.

"Other things that could never fit in a pickle jar," Darlene added, and everyone laughed once again.

~ THE END ~

The True Story:

 The story I just had the pleasure of sharing with you is entirely true. Of course, as the writer, I added little details from my own imagination. Old Mrs. Estes, the frozen stockings, and even the pickle jar are my own additions. However, Eddie, Darlene, and Ocy are all very much real, as is their mother, their little church and the heartfelt adventure this story is about. Darlene really did have cardboard in her shoes on their way to church that morning and they really did make a game out of choosing silverware!

This story was first written for a missionary letter. Eddie has sent letters to missionary families every single month since 1980

and continues to do so today. The letters are meant to encourage the whole family, and Eddie often includes funny stories. Today, there are over five hundred missionaries on the mailing list! The missionary families loved the story of Easter offering so much, it was published online, which is how I first came to read it. I was so moved by the story, I wrote a letter to Eddie and asked her if I could turn it into a book. I didn't know that, a couple of years later, I would get to travel from my home in Texas to meet Eddie in Washington State. She was so wonderful to talk to and so inspiring to learn from.

Since saving up pennies and dimes for the poor family in her church, Eddie has grown up, gotten married and created her own family. She and her husband Phil dated for six days before marrying, and have now been married for sixty-three years! Eddie and Phil have twelve children, eleven of which were adopted. They were foster parents from 1962 to 2002 and, during that time, opened their home to seventy-seven children!

During our conversation, Eddie told me, "I never thought I was poor, but looking back, now I know. We were always so happy, I wanted other kids to experience the happy home life I had."

Phil and Eddie still live in Washington, still are very involved in church, with missionaries and ministries for orphans. Eddie still writes her letters to over 500 foreign missionaries every month. They have thirteen children, twenty-eight grandchildren, thirty-six great-grandchildren and four great-great-grandchildren, a happy marriage and a love for strawberry milkshakes.

About the Authoress/Illustrator:

Caroline Kraft is the third of nine children and could easily relate to Eddie's comments about growing up in a busy, happy home. She remains at that home, affectionately called Eyrie Park, today. Five of Caroline's siblings came to her through international adoption. Caroline loves to write, doodle, watch old movies, see the world and squeeze her nephew. She lives in Texas with her parents and several siblings.

This is her first book to write or illustrate. She blogs at carolinerosekraft.com

This book was made possible by:

Rachelle Rea of rachellerea.com, editor.

Roseanna White of roseannawhite.com, cover designer, and formatter.

The Patmos Mastermind Team for constant support, prayer and guidance.

And the faithful readers of my blog since 2007. Y'all make it all worthwhile.